ORNAMENTAL
KNOTS *for*
BEADED
JEWELLERY

Dedication

This book is dedicated to the memory of
our dear friend Miriam Mirvish.

A free spirit.

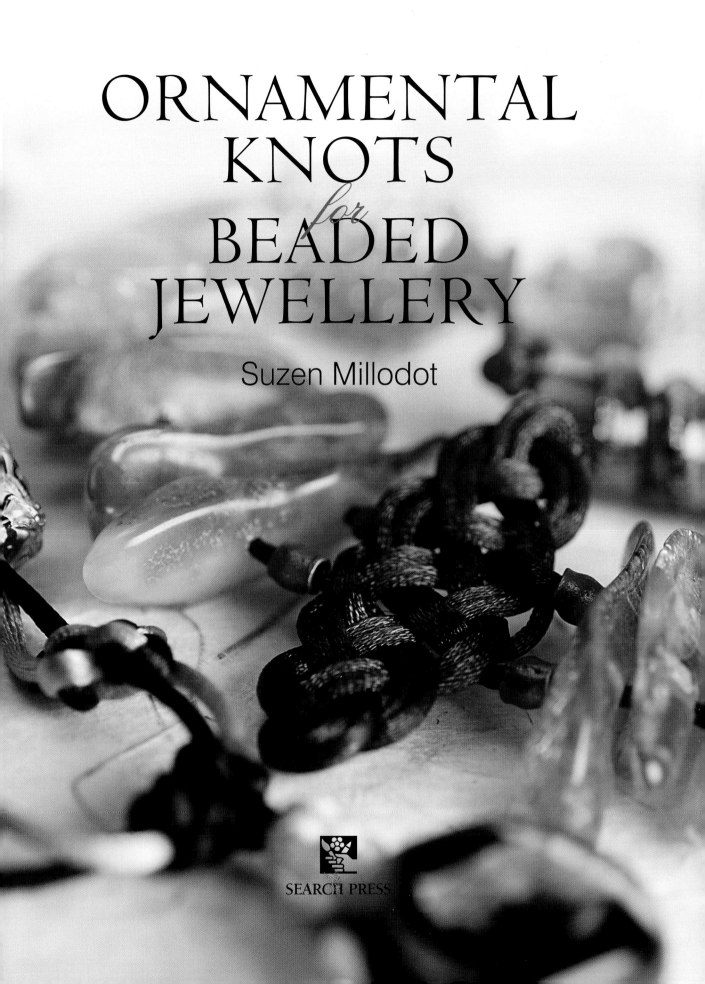

ORNAMENTAL
KNOTS
for
BEADED
JEWELLERY

Suzen Millodot

SEARCH PRESS

First published in Great Britain 2008

Search Press Limited
Wellwood, North Farm Road,
Tunbridge Wells, Kent TN2 3DR

Text copyright © Suzen Millodot 2008

Photographs by Debbie Patterson at Search Press studios

Photographs and design copyright © Search Press Ltd 2008

ISBN: 978-1-84448-248-1

The Publishers and author can accept no responsibility for
any consequences arising from the information, advice or
instructions given in this publication.

Readers are permitted to reproduce any of the items in this
book for their personal use, or for the purposes of selling for
charity, free of charge and without the prior permission of the
Publishers. Any use of the items for commercial purposes is not
permitted without the prior permission of the Publishers.

Suppliers

If you have difficulty in obtaining any of the materials and
equipment mentioned in this book, then please visit the Search
Press website for details of suppliers: www.searchpress.com

You are also invited to visit the author's website:
www.ornamental-knots.com

Publisher's note

All the step-by-step photographs in this book feature
the author, Suzen Millodot, demonstrating how to tie
ornamental knots and how to make jewellery using
ornamental knots. No models have been used.

Printed in Malaysia

ACKNOWLEDGEMENTS

*Special thanks to Black Dragon Crafts in Wales for supplying
the beautiful Celtic beads used in some of the projects in this
book; to Ray Skene of Celtic Glass in Wales for making many
of the lovely lampwork beads that feature in this book; to
Rachelle Goldreich for the handmade glass water nymph and
beautiful lampwork beads; to Robin of www.satincord.com
who supplied the 1mm satin cords; to Marlene Minhas for
the fused glass beads; and to Todd and Sherry Greer of Lady
Penguinevere Designs in Austin, Texas for the 'Guinevere'
Celtic knot design.*

*Last but not least I am indebted to my husband Michel for
his unwavering support and encouragement.*

CONTENTS

INTRODUCTION 6

MATERIALS AND EQUIPMENT 8
  Cords
  Beads and pendants
  Findings
  Other items

PREPARING CORDS 12
  Calculating lengths of cord
  Preparing cord ends
  Dyeing cords
  Tying knots

BUTTON KNOT NECKLACE 16

PINEAPPLE KNOT BRACELET 22

PHOENIX TAIL NECKLACE 28

GUINEVERE'S NECKLACE 34

EPAULETTE KNOT BRACELET 40

FIRECRACKER KNOT EARRINGS 46

PIPA KNOT EARRINGS 52

MACRAMÉ NECKLACE 56

FOUR-LEAVED CLOVER
NECKLACE 64

DRAGONFLY BROOCH 72

INDEX 80

INTRODUCTION

Sometimes I think that I have not chosen knots, but that they have chosen me! Ever since I saw my first ornamental knot I have been utterly fascinated by their individuality: they are small and self-contained, they are handmade without the need for elaborate equipment, and their intricate patterns have an air of confidence and self-importance which I find very beguiling. They have a fascinating history and folklore all of their own. When I discover a new knot that I like, it does not leave me in peace until I have learned how to make it and combine it with beads to create a lovely piece of jewellery. Carefully chosen knots and beads can enhance each other beautifully!

Knots are as old as mankind. As man migrated across the world and travelled ceaselessly from place to place, he took his knots and knotting skills with him. Sailors used practical knots for many purposes aboard ship, but in their spare time the only thing they had available to them was rope and string, so, as well as tying functional knots, they used them to create very attractive decorative knots. They called them 'fancy knots'.

Many of the same knots can be found in different cultures with a different name in each because there have been a lot of cross-cultural exchanges. The best known one is the macramé knot called the Josephine knot, also called the double coin knot by the Chinese, and known as the Carrick bend by sailors. There are other knots, too numerous to list here, that are known by several different names.

As well as fancy knots there are two main types of purely ornamental knots that have never had any simple useful function (with the exception of the button knot) except to be beautiful and decorative, and perhaps to adorn other items. They are Chinese knots and Celtic knots.

The Chinese developed silk, and their intricate decorative knots were originally tied with silk cords. Today, many centuries later, they are still used in the same way as gifts to represent love and affection, and as decorations to celebrate nature and all the good things in life.

The Celtic monks devised incredibly intricate knot patterns which were mainly used to decorate other objects in stone-carvings and on paper, but it is thought very unlikely that they were ever tied into real three-dimensional knots.

It is interesting to note that both the Chinese and the ancient Celts used knots to represent exactly the same aspects of life and nature; such as the continuity and eternal cycle of life; the contrasts of dark and light, winter and summer, male and female; the concept of balance and harmony; and the interconnection of all things in the natural world. You can find out more about the history and folklore of the different knots in more detail in my previous books on Chinese and Celtic knots.

This book includes some Chinese knots, some hand-tied Celtic knots, and some fancy knots, and shows you in detail how to make them and combine them with beads and pendants to make very unusual and stylish jewellery.

Opposite:
Lampwork beads by Rachelle Goldreich on a necklace of macramé square knots and spiral knots.

MATERIALS AND EQUIPMENT

Cords

There is a far greater range of types of cords available now than when I started to make decorative knots, and it is much easier to find them. However, for many of us it will still be necessary to buy them by mail. One advantage of using the internet and mail order catalogues is that there is often more information available about the products on the website or in the catalogues, allowing you to plan and decide what you need in your own time at home.

The most important feature of the cord used for ornamental knots is that it should be firm: not be too limp, nor too stiff, but somewhere in between. To test this, make a loop with the cord. It should hold the loop firmly without flopping, but it should not be so stiff that you cannot change the shape when it becomes necessary.

In the projects in this book I have used 2mm satin cord, some 1mm satin cord, 1mm and 1.5mm leather cord, and braided cord in various thicknesses.

Satin cord is excellent for decorative knots as it is firm, easy to handle, slightly shiny and can stand the handling and pulling that knot tying requires. There are two types available, one made from nylon and the other from rayon. I prefer the nylon as it is less slippery and the end can be melted for a neat finish.

Leather cord is not so forgiving because it does not share these qualities. It is fine for Celtic style knots which do not need very much pulling about, but some Chinese knots are more demanding, and leather cord is not really suitable.

Braided cord is a pleasure to use as it holds the knot well and is not slippery.

All the cords have some advantages and disadvantages and you must decide which qualities are needed for the particular project that you have in mind.

A selection of cords.

Beads and pendants

The choice of beads available now is quite mind-boggling! For knotting, it is not possible to use beads which have very small holes, so this does narrow the choice a little. Beads are available in so many different materials, wood, semi-precious stones, ceramics, polymer clay, silver, pewter, plastic, fabric, glass and even felt and paper.

    One of the best types of bead for knotting is handmade fused glass and lampwork beads. These days there are many glass artists making wonderful colourful glass beads that team perfectly with knotting cords as they have nice large even holes, and the smooth vibrant glass looks so good with satin and braided cords in matching or complementary colours. There are bead fairs where you can find all sorts of beads, charity shops for unusual old beads, many bead shops have sprung up in small towns, and there are numerous mail order companies tempting us with a vast array of all types of beads. They can be very addictive and you will find yourself looking out for beads wherever you go!

Check that the beads you use have holes large enough to be suitable for the cords you use, and note that the projects in this book sometimes require you to be able to thread two cords through a bead.

Findings

Knotted jewellery does not need as many findings as regular strung-beaded necklaces do, as the adjustable sliding button knot is such a versatile finish. However when findings are needed you must make sure that the holes in the closures are large enough to thread the cords through, and also that the weight and appearance of the closure is suitable for the beads you have used: large beads need a more substantial closure and smaller beads need a smaller, more delicate clasp or toggle closure. Findings are available from the same sources as beads and cords that I have described above.

Make sure that the findings you use are suitable. More 'chunky' clasps look better with cords and knots. The findings need to have suitably large holes as well.

9

Other items

Scissors These should be very sharp to give you a neat end to the cords for threading through beads. Cords cut on the diagonal are easier to thread.

PVA glue This easily available white craft glue dries clear and is used to stiffen the ends of the cords. As it dries it hardens the end of the cord, which can then be used like a needle to thread the cord through the beads. It can also be diluted (ten parts water to one part glue) to brush on to the back of a knot to stiffen it slightly and keep the loops in place. It darkens the cord a little so I try to avoid using it on the front of the knot.

Paint brush This is used to brush the PVA glue on to the ends of the cords, and to brush diluted glue on to finished knots to stiffen them slightly.

Lighter A cigarette lighter is very useful for sealing the ends of synthetic cords neatly and unobtrusively in knotted jewellery. The cord end should be put into the flame for a very short time (a fraction of a second). This is just long enough to seal it to give a very neat finish to the knot, but not so long that the end of the cord becomes an ugly brown knob.

Thread zapper Very good for finishing jewellery, this cuts and heat-seals synthetic cords with one 'zap'. I don't use it for thicker cords as it uses up the batteries too quickly, but it's great for thinner, more delicate cords. It is also very accurate.

Pins Used to hold the partially finished knot in place as you work out what the next move should be. They are very helpful for holding the shape of the curves as you work. Old-fashioned T pins are too coarse, and will spoil the cords, so use glass-headed sewing pins.

Tweezers I do not generally use tweezers, except to pull cords through small spaces, but they can occasionally be really useful for difficult-to-reach corners.

Instant glue gel This comes in a dispenser which allows you to put a tiny drop of superglue gel exactly where you want it, and it does not spread and spoil your work. It holds the ends of the completed knot in place and prevents the knot from coming apart during handling later on. It is less visible than stitches and much faster!

Epoxy glue You will only need this strong glue occasionally, but nevertheless it is very useful for attaching pins to completed knots to make brooches.

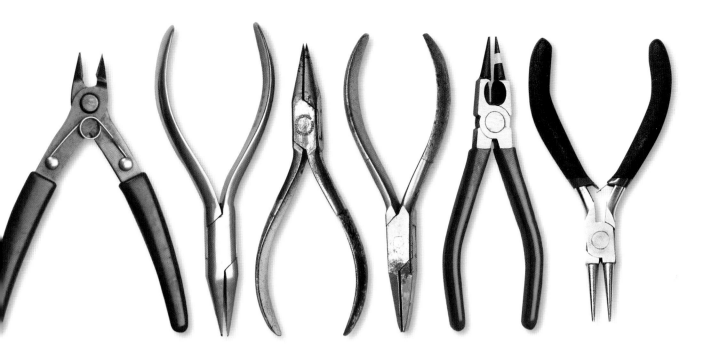

Bead reamer This tool is invaluable for smoothing and slightly enlarging difficult holes in beads. In some cheaper glass beads the unsightly white powdery releasing agent has not been cleaned out of the bead hole. The reamer will remove this. However, when used for this purpose the reamer must be regularly cleaned with an old toothbrush to remain effective.

Cork mat I like to use my cork mat on an adjustable laptray as I can angle the mat towards me in order to work on the knot more comfortably. The cork mat allows you to position the pins in the loops and curves of a knot and alter the placement as the knot develops. The cork is sturdy and lasts for years.

Needle A large-holed needlepoint needle with a blunt rounded end is occasionally useful when you need to thread the cord back through a button knot to finish a necklace or bracelet.

Pliers and wire cutters These are not often needed for knotted jewellery, but when you need to use a headpin or an eyepin to thread through a small-holed bead (to make an earring for example), wire cutters are needed to cut the wire and pliers to make a loop on the end of the pin. I have also used pliers to grip and pull a difficult cord through a small space.

From left: wire cutters, two pairs of needle-nosed pliers, wide flat-nosed pliers, large round-ended pliers, small round-ended pliers.

Clear nail polish Clear nail polish is very useful for stiffening cord ends quickly, as it dries hard in a few minutes. It is great when you are using beads with nice large smooth regular holes. However, if you know that you are going to have a difficult time getting your cord through the bead holes (using semi-precious stones for example, or two or more cords through one bead), it is better to use the PVA glue as it gives a much harder and stiffer end to your cord.

Tape measure To measure the length of the cord before starting your project.

A cork mat attached to a laptray.

PREPARING CORDS

The best way to thread a cord through a bead is to make the end of the cord stiff so that it acts like a needle. Two methods are described opposite.

Calculating lengths of cord

The following tables will help you work out how much cord to use. It is surprising how much cord is needed for decorative knots, almost always more than you had imagined! I find that as a very general rule three metres (118in) of cord is about right for most necklaces with button knots. If you find a beautiful cord you must have (before you have worked out what to use it for) then buy at least three metres; any less would probably be too short. It is better to have too much than too little cord.

Extra cord is always needed at the end of a necklace to be able to tie the last button knot, so an allowance must be made for that too. When making a necklace with more complicated knots then four metres is a good length to start with.

Necklace lengths

The following table lists the average length of cord you will need for different types of necklace.

Choker	40cm	(16in)
Necklace with fastener	45cm	(18in)
Necklace without fastener	70cm	(28in)

Cord lengths for knots

The following table shows the approximate length of **2mm** cord required to tie single knots.

Button knot	8.5cm	(3½in)
Sliding button knot	9.5cm	(3¾in)
Double button knot	25cm	(10in)

The following table shows the approximate length of **1mm** cord required to tie single knots.

Button knot	5.5cm	(2⅛in)
Sliding button knot	5.7cm	(2¼in)
Double button knot	15cm	(6in)

The following table shows how to determine the total length of **2mm** cord required to make an 80cm (32in) necklace with one double button knot, ten single button knots and two sliding button knots.

Length of necklace	80cm	(32in)
Double button knot	25cm	(10in)
Ten button knots	85cm	(34in)
Two sliding knots	19cm	(7½in)
Allowance for tying the sliding knots	60cm	(24in)
Total length	269cm	(107½in)

Note that it is better to have too much cord than too little, so I would add a small allowance for possible additions and cut a 3m (118in) length of cord.

Preparing cord ends

Cord ends will need to be prepared before they are used. Clear nail polish is easy to use and dries in about fifteen minutes and is good for smooth holes. PVA glue takes longer to dry, overnight is best, but it dries much harder than nail polish, so it is better for more difficult holes.

You can even make the end of the cord thinner by cutting a small sliver off the side of the stiffened end so that it goes through the bead hole more easily. Once it has appeared on the opposite side of the bead you can grip the end and pull the rest through (your pliers will be useful here). A 2mm satin cord will actually go through a hole which looks smaller than 2mm, if you have prepared the end carefully.

Cutting and stiffening 2mm cords with scissors and glue before starting

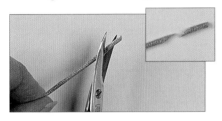

1. Use a pair of sharp scissors to cut across the cord at an angle near the end to make a point.

2. Dip a paintbrush into PVA glue and brush the end of the cord.

3. Turn the cord over and brush PVA on the other side. Leave to dry overnight. This makes a stiff 'needle' for threading.

Cutting and stiffening 2mm cords with scissors and nail varnish

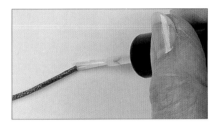

Tip

Nail varnish makes for a less stiff 'needle' than PVA glue, but it is very quick to dry and fine for beads with large smooth holes.

1. Use a pair of sharp scissors to cut across the cord at an angle near the end to make a point.

2. Use the applicator to apply nail varnish to the end of the cord. Allow to dry for fifteen minutes.

Cutting and sealing 1mm cords with a zapper to finish

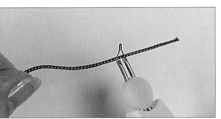

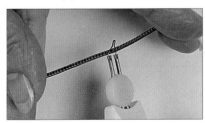

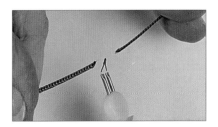

1. Feed an inch or two of cord through the cutting wire of the zapper.

2. Grip the loose end between the first two fingers of your left hand.

3. Hold the on/off button down and gently pull the zapper through to cut and seal the cord.

Dyeing cords

Although cords are available in many colours, it is sometimes impossible to find the exact shade that will complement your beads. Multi-purpose dyes are easily available and are fadeproof under ordinary circumstances and come in many colours. You can use these to dye white cords to a rich colour, or deepen a very pale cord to a darker shade.

It is very easy to dye cords in the microwave oven, as they don't take up a lot of space or need large containers.

Nylon and rayon (also known as acetate or viscose) dye easily, as do wool, cotton, linen and silk. Polyester and polypropylene do not take ordinary dyes, but a cotton polyester mix will dye to a pale shade. Cotton piping cord takes dye very well, but not waxed cotton or linen.

Although this is not strictly dyeing, I have very successfully given a too-bright white nylon cord an antique feel by dipping it into a mug of strong hot tea (no milk!) for five minutes (see page 71 for a picture of the piece).

Method

You will need a large heatproof glass jug, a spoon, an old newspaper to protect the kitchen counter and rubber gloves. Wear old clothes or an apron. Wrap the cord around your hand to make a loose hank and secure it with a small piece of cord loosely tied around it.

1. Put 600ml (20 fl oz or 2½ cups) of very hot water into the jug.

2. Add ¼ tsp of dye and ½ tsp salt. Stir to make sure the dye powder dissolves completely.

3. Immerse the cord into the dye solution. Stir gently to make sure the cord is thoroughly saturated with dye solution.

4. Place in the microwave oven. Since ovens vary so much, it is not possible to give the power needed for your particular oven to keep the solution simmering. It will be a low or medium setting as you definitely do not want the solution to boil over.

5. After five minutes, check the colour and stir the dye. Most manufacturers recommend dyeing for twenty minutes, but it seems to dye much more quickly in the microwave.

6. When you have achieved the colour you want (do not forget it looks much darker when wet) remove the cord from the solution, rinse it and leave it still wound up flat on the newspaper to dry.

A selection of hand-dyed cords.

TYING KNOTS

Here we are using a very well-known and elegant knot, the Josephine knot, as an example of how to tie and tighten. This knot is used in the epaulette knot bracelet on page 44.

Weaving the knot

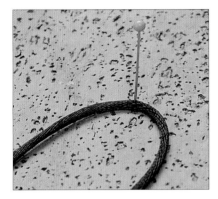

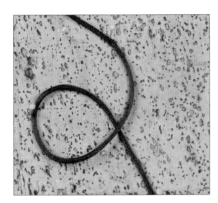

1. Pin your cord to a cork mat, making sure that the pin goes through the cord. (Note that leather cord should not be pinned. See page 41 for how to secure leather cord.)

2. As you begin to make the knot, follow the diagrams carefully. Pin through the cord where convenient in order to hold the loops in place.

3. Continue the knot, making sure that you take the cord under and over according to the diagrams. Pin where convenient until the knot is loosely completed.

Tightening the knot

1. For a simple knot such as this example, remove all of the pins except for the pin marking the centre of the knot. This acts as an anchor.

2. With the pins removed, gently tug parts of the knot to tighten it, starting from the centre. Ease the cord through in small movements.

3. Continue the gradual process of tightening. Try to keep the tension even throughout the knot, rather than getting one isolated part tight. When you are satisfied with the knot, remove the anchoring pin.

BUTTON KNOT NECKLACE

The Chinese have been using these perfectly round little knots as buttons for centuries, hence their name. In Chinese Buddhism their endless pattern represents the eternal cycle of life, and it means exactly the same in Celtic mythology.

In knotted jewellery its round shape is perfect for hiding the ends of cords, so as well as being elegant it is very useful. Button knots and beads combine beautifully and enhance each other well, as you can see in the necklace featured here.

The button knot is also incredibly useful for making adjustable necklaces with the sliding button knot, also featured in this project.

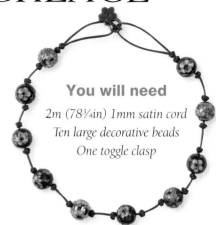

You will need

2m (78¾in) 1mm satin cord
Ten large decorative beads
One toggle clasp

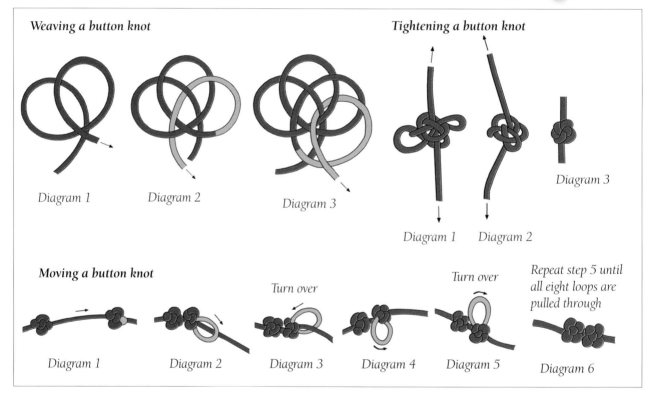

Weaving a button knot

Diagram 1

Diagram 2

Diagram 3

Tightening a button knot

Diagram 1

Diagram 2

Diagram 3

Moving a button knot

Diagram 1

Diagram 2

Turn over

Diagram 3

Diagram 4

Turn over

Diagram 5

Repeat step 5 until all eight loops are pulled through

Diagram 6

Note that exactly the same method of tying a button knot around another cord is used to finish a necklace, although it will not necessarily slide.

Tip

Sliding knots can be slid back and forth to adjust the length of a necklace. To do so, tie a button knot around the cord of the <u>opposing</u> side of a necklace, as shown.

Sliding button knots used with a fastener. This knot is tied around the cord on the <u>same</u> side of the necklace. This method also makes your necklaces adjustable.

1. Stiffen the ends of the cords (see page 13), then thread a bead on to one end of the cord, as though threading a needle.

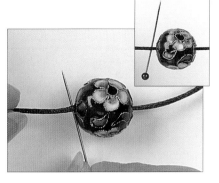

2. Fold the cord in half to find the halfway point, then run the bead down the cord until it sits in the centre. Push a pin through the cord to the left of the bead to hold it in place.

3. Make a loop to the right of the bead, taking the cord over itself.

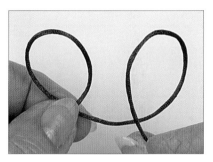

4. Holding the first loop between your thumb and index finger, make a second loop to the right.

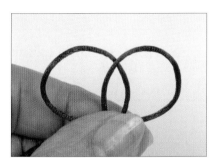

5. Take the second loop between your thumb and index finger, on top of the first loop. See diagram 1.

6. Take the right-hand end of the cord down through the loop on the right-hand side.

7. Take the end back up through the area where the two loops overlap one another.

8. Take the end down through the loop on the left and ease the cord through on the right-hand side just enough to make a third loop as shown. See diagram 2.

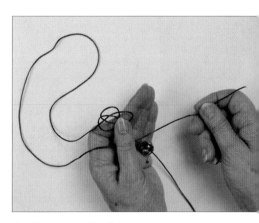

9. Keeping hold of the knot in your left hand, take the end through the gap between your left thumb and forefinger as shown.

10. Pull the cord through, then take the end down through the third (new) loop.

11. Bring the end up through the lower part of the central loop, just above your left thumb.

12. Pull the cord through to begin to secure the knot. See diagram 3.

13. Release the loops from between your finger and thumb and take both ends between your fingers; making sure the left cord is behind the knot and the right cord is in front as shown.

14. Gently pull the cords to tighten the knot. Guide the knot to lean towards the right side. This ensures the knot will tighten correctly.

15. Identify a large loop, look for the point it re-enters the knot and pull the next loop through until the large loop lies flat against the knot.

16. Continue pulling the loops through until the button knot has taken shape.

17. Once tightened, the knot will finish about 10cm (4in) from the bead, so it needs to be moved next to the bead. Follow the cord from the bead to where it enters and leaves the knot, and pull it out while slipping the knot down towards the bead. See the diagrams on page 16.

Tip
Always hold the knot in your left hand and pull the loop towards you when tightening.

18. Once the knot is adjacent to the bead, tighten it as described in steps 14–16.

19. Turn the necklace round and remove the pin, then make a second button knot on the other side of the bead.

20. Make another button knot to the right of the previous one, and move it down until it is a thumb's width away from the previous knot.

21. Thread on a blue bead and hold it in place with a second button knot.

22. Repeat this process to secure four more beads on the right and four more beads on the left as shown.

23. Thread the loop of the closure on to the left-hand end of the cord, leaving it 20cm (8in) from the end.

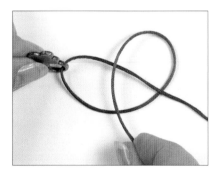

24. Now you will make a button knot around the main cord. Place the clasp on the left side, then take the loose end of the cord underneath itself and round to make two overlapping loops.

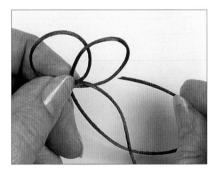

25. Hold the loops in your thumb and forefinger, then take the free end around and underneath the holding cord as shown, ready to go into the loop on the right.

26. Take the end down through the right loop, up through the overlapping part and down through the left-hand loop. This makes a new, third loop on the right.

27. Take the end through the gap between your left thumb and forefinger behind the holding cord again, then down through the new loop and up through the middle opening above your thumb.

Tip

Single button knots can be trimmed and made into a bead, then threaded on to a necklace or bracelet in exactly the same way as a regular bead.

28. Tighten the knot a little then move it along the cord (see page 16) so that the loop closure is in the right place before fully tightening the knot.

Tip

When making a sliding button knot, the cord should always be behind the holding cord when going upwards, and in front of the holding cord when going down.

Note

This completes a sliding button knot. This knot is identical to a button knot except that it is tied around another cord. This means that the knot can be slid up and down along the cord, making it very versatile and useful.

29. Tighten the sliding button knot in the same way as the button knot.

30. Secure the toggle to the other end of the cord in the same way.

31. Trim and seal the ends coming from the sliding button knots, following the instructions on page 13.

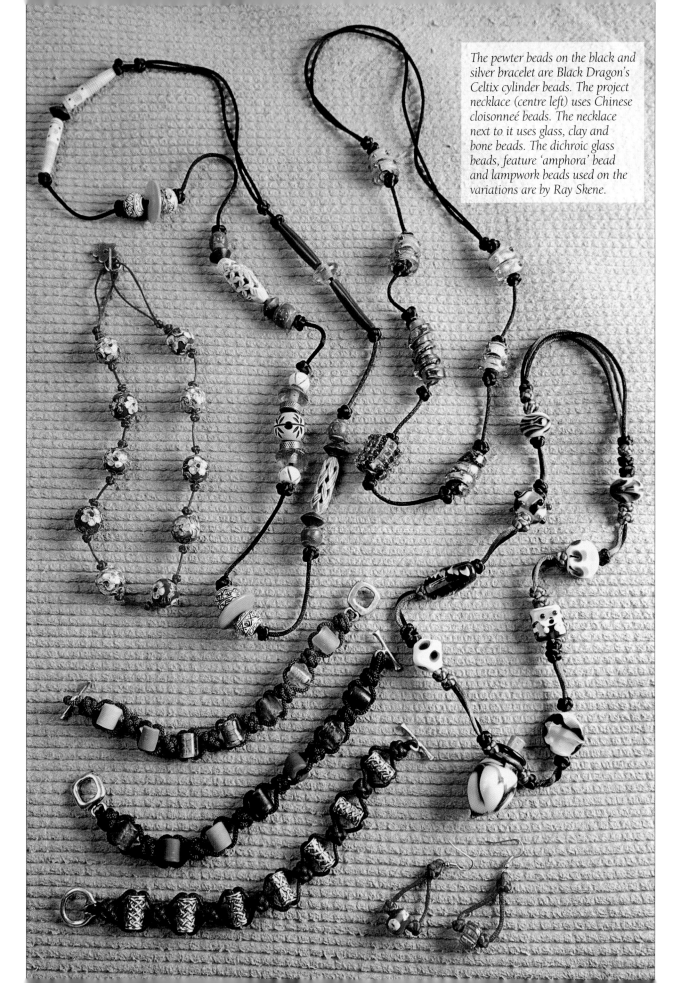

The pewter beads on the black and silver bracelet are Black Dragon's Celtix cylinder beads. The project necklace (centre left) uses Chinese cloisonneé beads. The necklace next to it uses glass, clay and bone beads. The dichroic glass beads, feature 'amphora' bead and lampwork beads used on the variations are by Ray Skene.

PINEAPPLE KNOT BRACELET

The pineapple knot is an extended button knot, and is also called an extended diamond knot, but pineapple knot sounds much nicer!

This knot will be easier to follow if you are already familiar with making the button knot. It looks difficult at first, but once you have made one or two the method will begin to make more sense to you. It is made with the two ends of the cord as if they are separate cords.

The tightening differs from the button knot: instead of simply pulling the loops through around the knot, you also work up and down the knot as you pull the loops through, and tighten each end of the cord separately.

The knot looks very attractive and interesting when combined with beads, as you can see in this bracelet.

You will need

One toggle clasp
2.5m (98in) 2mm satin cord
Celtic beads: two star-shaped, two 'Cyfrin dragon's eye', two 'Cyfrin balls', one large ball and one square

Weaving a pineapple knot

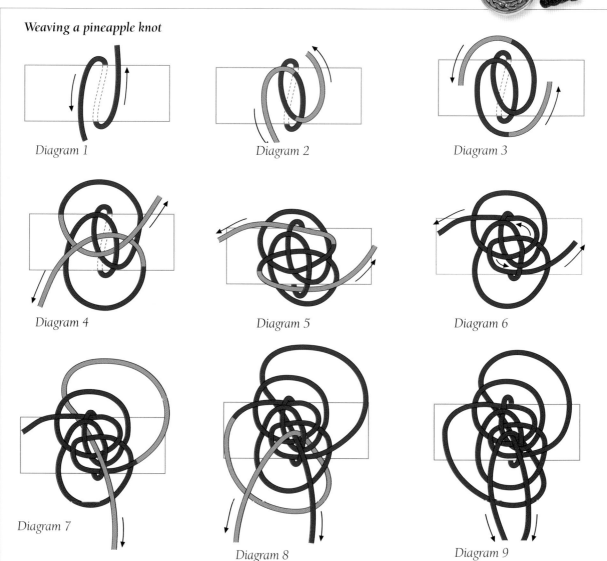

Diagram 1

Diagram 2

Diagram 3

Diagram 4

Diagram 5

Diagram 6

Diagram 7

Diagram 8

Diagram 9

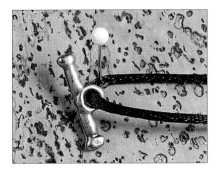

1. Thread the toggle to the middle of the cord and pin the cord in place on the corkboard.

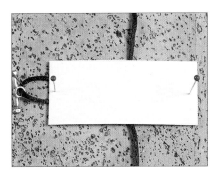

2. Cut a piece of card 12 x 4cm (4¾ x 1½in) and pin it on top of the cord close to the toggle. Take one end of the cord upwards and the other end downwards.

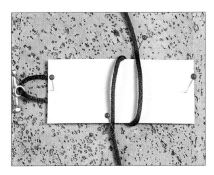

3. Fold the ends of the cords over the card and pin them as shown. See diagram 1.

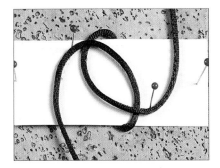

4. Remove the pins, overlay the cords as shown and repin. See diagram 2.

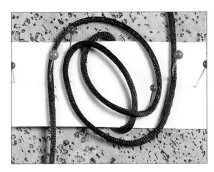

5. Spiral the cords once around the new pins and pin each in place halfway up the card. See diagram 3.

6. Take the end on the right, take it over the first two cords to its left, under the third and over the fourth as shown.

7. Mirror the action with the other end of the cord, taking it over two cords to its right, under the third and over the fourth. See diagram 4.

8. Take the same end back from right to left through the middle loop at the top as shown (it is the loop that appears from under the white card).

9. Carefully pull the cord through to make a loop at the top right.

10. Mirror the action with the other end of the cord, threading it from the left to right. See diagram 5.

11. Pull both cords slightly tighter to make the shape shown above. See diagram 6.

12. Take the free end that is now on the right and loop it round the top of the knot, before taking it under all of the cords and bringing it up in the central hole. Pull the cord down over the rest of the cords (see inset). See diagram 7.

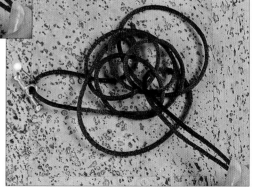

13. Mirror the process with the other free end, taking it down and round to the right then under the cords, up through the centre and upwards over the other cords. See diagram 8.

14. Take hold of both free ends and take them downwards. Carefully remove all of the pins except the one holding the toggle in place. See diagram 9.

15. Carefully slide the card out from the knot.

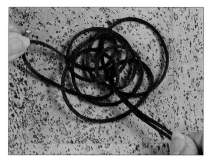

16. Remove the last pin, pick up the middle of the cord with your left hand, just below the toggle, and take the free ends in your right hand.

17. Gently pull your hands apart to begin to form the knot.

18. Starting with the largest loose loop, even out the tension through the knot by working up and down the knot until it looks like this. This is a tightened pineapple knot.

19. When the knot has taken shape, move it up towards the toggle in the centre of the cord in the same way as the button knot (see page 13).

20. Thread a star-shaped bead on to both ends of the cord and move it up to the pineapple knot.

21. Secure the bead in place by making a second pineapple knot in the same way as the first and tightening it next to the bead.

22. Put a Cyfrin ball bead inside a Cyfrin dragon's eye bead. Treating this as one bead, thread it on the ends of the cord, move it up adjacent to the second pineapple knot, then secure it in place with a third pineapple knot.

23. Repeat this process with a square bead, a second two-part bead, a second star bead and a large ball bead, separating and securing them with pineapple knots.

Tip

You can add another bead and knot if you want a longer bracelet.

24. Make a loose pineapple knot next to the final round bead (inset), then take one end of the cord through the toggle loop. Take the other end through the loop in the other direction. This makes the cords much less likely to loosen.

25. Pull the ends through until the toggle loop is near the loose knot, then feed one end into and through the knot.

26. Feed the other end through the knot, then pull both ends tight. Tighten the knot around the cords. Secure the ends where they leave the knot with a spot of instant glue gel.

27. Trim and seal the ends of the cords to finish the bracelet.

Opposite:

This knot works really well for necklaces, as shown by the three variations here. The top left variation uses lampwork beads made by Ray Skene, while the Celtic beads on the project bracelet are from Black Dragon's range. The necklace on the top right uses Greek clay beads and gold beads from Black Dragon, while the lower right necklace uses porcelain beads and Greek clay beads.

PHOENIX TAIL NECKLACE

This necklace is made of chain knots, made with two cords instead of the more usual one. This makes it much more stable and attractive. A pendant which is stunning on its own does not need the addition of a lot of knots, as they could detract from its appearance. The phoenix tail is beautiful but subtle, and will complement virtually any pendant.

Here I use a beautiful pendant in lapis lazuli and silver made by Native Americans, from Santa Fe, New Mexico.

I like the chain when made with two cords of the same colour, but it can also be made with two different colours. This has the advantage that it shows off the construction of the chain very nicely, and it is a great way to make a cord of the necklace the focal point.

You will need

5.5m (216½in) silver-grey 2mm satin cord

Hook and eye clasp

Two tubular beads with very large holes

Feature pendant with bail

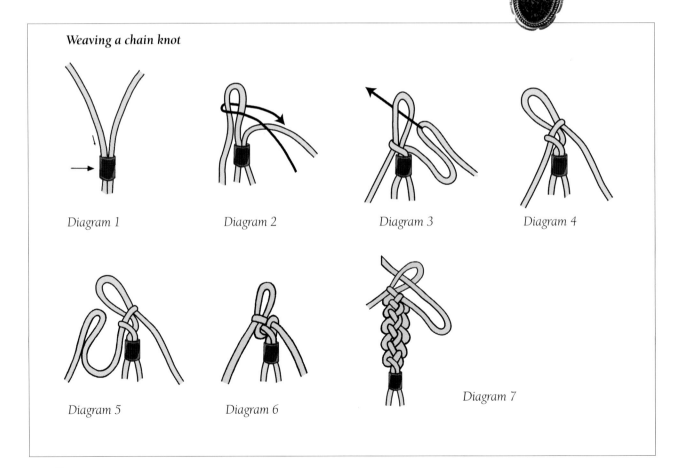

Weaving a chain knot

Diagram 1

Diagram 2

Diagram 3

Diagram 4

Diagram 5

Diagram 6

Diagram 7

1. Find the centre point of your cord, thread the hook and run it down the cord to this point.

2. Make a button knot around the cord next to the hook, following the instructions on pages 19 and the diagram on page 16.

3. Put both of the ends of the cord through a tubular bead and run it up to the knot.

4. Make a loop with the cord on the left-hand side. Hold the loop next to the bead with your left hand as shown.

5. Take the end of the cord on the right and wrap it round the loop. See diagram 2.

6. Hold the wrapped part tightly and make a second loop with the cord on the right-hand side.

7. Take the new loop through the first loop from front to back. See diagram 3.

8. Gently pull the first loop closed around the second loop. See diagram 4.

9. Ease the resultant knot tight.

10. Make a third loop with the cord on the left. See diagram 5.

11. Take the third loop through the second loop from front to back. See diagram 6.

12. Pull the second loop closed around the third loop.

13. Make a fourth loop with the cord on the right, take it through the third and pull the third loop tight. You can now see the chain knot pattern start to emerge.

14. Continue working chain knots until the work measures 32cm (12½in). Leave a loop at the end.

Detail of chain knots.

15. Take the right-hand end of the cord through the loop. See diagram 7.

16. Pull the loop tight around the cord. (Note: if your pendant has a small bail or loop, add it on to the chain at this point.)

17. Thread a tubular bead with both ends of the cord and run it down to the end of the chain knots.

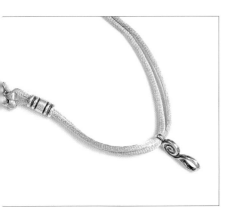

18. Thread the eye of the clasp on to the ends and run it down to approximately 10cm (4in) from the bead to allow space for tying a button knot.

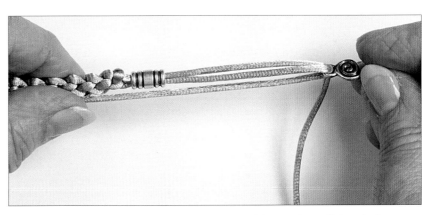

19. Use your left hand to hold one free end of the cord parallel with the cords leading from the knot.

20. Use the free end to tie a button knot around the other three cords.

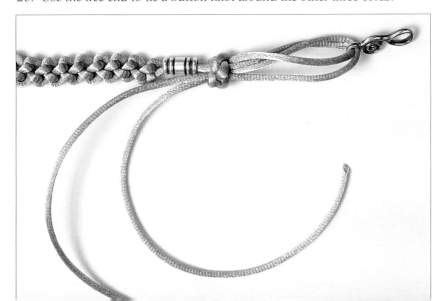

Note

Instructions for tying a button knot around other cords can be found on pages 19–20.

Tip

If you are right-handed, you will find it easier to turn the work from right to left before tying the knot.

21. Pull the extra cord through after moving the knot next to the bead.

22. Trim and seal the ends of the cord. Add an invisible spot of instant glue gel if needed.

23. Slip the bail and pendant on to the eye end of the cord and run it down to the central point to finish the necklace.

Opposite:

Try different colours to complement your feature pendant best. Clockwise from top left: turquoise and silver, black and gold porcelain, enamelled Gustav Klimt-inspired pendant, and the project necklace with blue lapis lazuli and silver. In the centre a fantasy water nymph bead by Rachelle Goldreich makes a beautiful pendant.

GUINEVERE'S NECKLACE

This lovely knot has inspired quite a number of people to start making Celtic knots. I received the design from Todd and Sherry Greer in Austin, Texas, who make hand-tied Celtic knotwork. They learnt this knot from Dave Love at a Renaissance fair.

Another name for the Guinevere knot could be the 'Renaissance knot' as it keeps re-appearing, tied in leather and different cords. It is great to know that so many people are now tying Celtic knots and making jewellery with them.

You will need

3m (118in) light red
2mm satin cord

3m (118in) dark red
2mm satin cord

One pendant with bail

Celtic beads: four bars and
two 'Cyfrin dragon's eye'

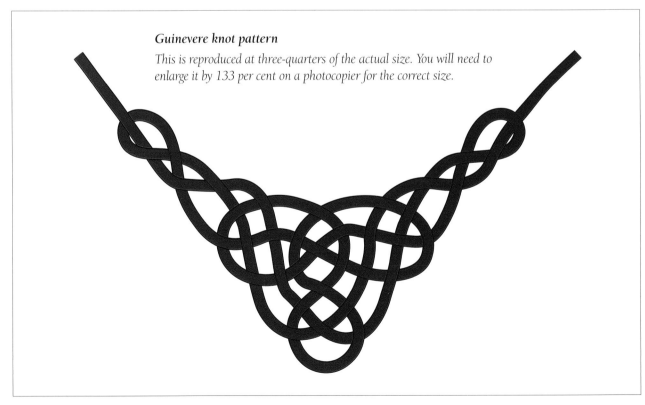

Guinevere knot pattern

This is reproduced at three-quarters of the actual size. You will need to enlarge it by 133 per cent on a photocopier for the correct size.

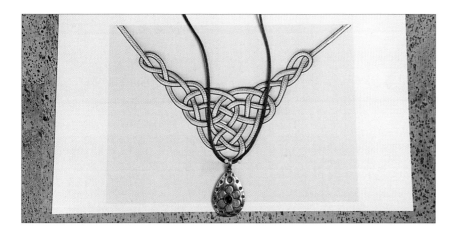

1. Photocopy the pattern and pin it to your cork mat. Thread the pendant on to the middle of the light red cord and pin it in place on either side of the pendant.

Tip

You can enlarge the pattern on a photocopier if you wish.

2. Starting with the end of the cord emerging from the right of the pendant, begin to lay the cord so that it follows where the pattern leads. Pin where necessary to keep the cord on the pattern.

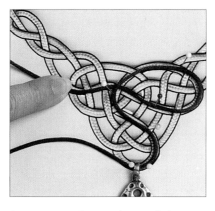

3. Continue laying the cord along the lines of the pattern. Where the pattern leads the cord back on itself, check whether the pattern indicates you to take the cord under or over itself to continue.

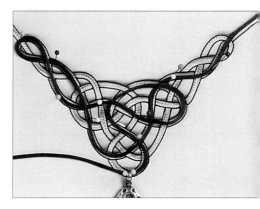

4. Work carefully around the pattern, making sure the cord goes under and over itself where appropriate. The pattern eventually leads the right-hand cord off to the top right corner. Secure it with a pin.

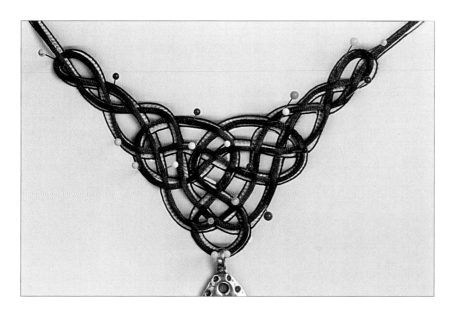

5. Follow the pattern in the other direction using the cord emerging from the left of the pendant. Pay careful attention to the 'unders and overs' where the cords cross each other.

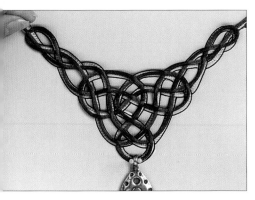

6. The triangle is now fairly stable, so you can remove most of the pins. If you feel the work moves too much, you can add a couple of extra pins to support it.

7. Thread the dark red cord on to the pendant and run it through until the central point of the cord is in the pendant. Pin it to secure it in place within the loop of the light red cord at the bottom.

8. Follow the pattern again, laying the right-hand end of the dark red cord down next to the light red cord. Make sure that the cords remain touching, but do not allow them to cross. When the cord reaches the top right corner, pin the cord to secure it in place.

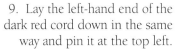

9. Lay the left-hand end of the dark red cord down in the same way and pin it at the top left.

10. Remove all but the pin next to the pendant and begin tightening the knot by pulling the loops away from the central point. Do not try to tighten too much at once as this can distort the shape.

11. Continue pulling the cords around the pattern, following the path in which the cords were laid down. Do not allow the light red and dark cords to cross at any point: keep them next to one another.

12. Notice how tightening enlarges a loop, which is then tightened by pulling it a short distance further along the design. This gradual process keeps everything aligned in the correct shape.

13. The piece will gradually get smaller as you tighten, so a stage-by-stage approach is best. Work around and around the cord until the knot is roughly half the size of the original pattern.

14. Remove the piece from the cork mat and pattern, then tie a button knot around the light red cord on the top left using the adjacent dark red cord.

15. Thread a bar bead on to both cords, slide it down to the button knot, then make a second button knot next to the bead with the light red cord knotted around the dark red cord.

16. Thread both cords through one side of a Cyfrin dragon's eye bead (see inset), then run it down to the second button knot. Make a third button knot by tying the light red cord around the dark red cord and move it down within the dragon's eye bead. Take the ends of the cords out of the other side of the bead. (See page 16 for how to move the button knot.)

17. Make a button knot above the bead using the light red cord around the dark red cord. Slip on a bar bead and then tie a sliding button knot using the dark red cord around the light red cord.

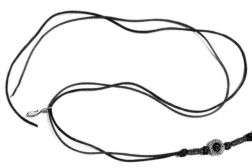

18. Thread both cords through the hook and run it down to approximately 15cm (6in) from the last button knot.

> **Note**
>
> *It is important to use and alternate both coloured cords to make the knots. If you use only one colour the knots will slide up and down and spoil the design.*

19. Using the free end of the light red cord, tie a sliding button knot around the other three cords. Move the knot up to the hook and then tighten.

20. Cut and seal the end of the light red cord.

21. Tie a sliding button knot around the other three cords using the free end of the dark red cord. Move the knot up to the hook and then tighten it. Cut and seal the dark red cord. You now have two sliding knots side by side which is more comfortable than a double button knot on the back of the neck. When moving them, hold both at the same time as if they were one.

22. Repeat this process using the cords on the right-hand side of the piece, substituting an eye for the hook when finishing.

Note

When there is a clasp in between the sliding knots, each sliding knot must be moved separately to adjust the length of the necklace.

Both can be moved at once if there is no clasp in between them.

Opposite:

The finished necklace is at the bottom right. The blue necklace to the left is made with a thick firm cord which keeps stable once knotted even though it is only a single cord, while the gold necklace uses leather cords and has a feature lampwork bead by Rachelle Goldreich.

EPAULETTE KNOT BRACELET

Traditionally an epaulette knot is a decoration worn on the shoulder of certain uniforms, especially military ones. However it also looks very good made with leather cord and combined with beads as you see in the bracelet here.

It is based on the Josephine knot (see page 15) extended on each side. Pay particular attention to the 'unders and overs' at the beginning as they do vary a little from the basic Josephine knot. Here the first leather cord starts at the top of the central knot and the second cord starts at the bottom of the knot. It is more difficult to tighten the knot as each cord goes in a different direction…but the results are well worth the effort!

You will need

Two 2m (78¾in) lengths of black 1mm leather cord

Four dichroic fused glass beads with parallel holes

One silver toggle clasp

Note

Any beads with two parallel holes (or even those with one central hole) will work with this method.

Weaving an epaulette knot

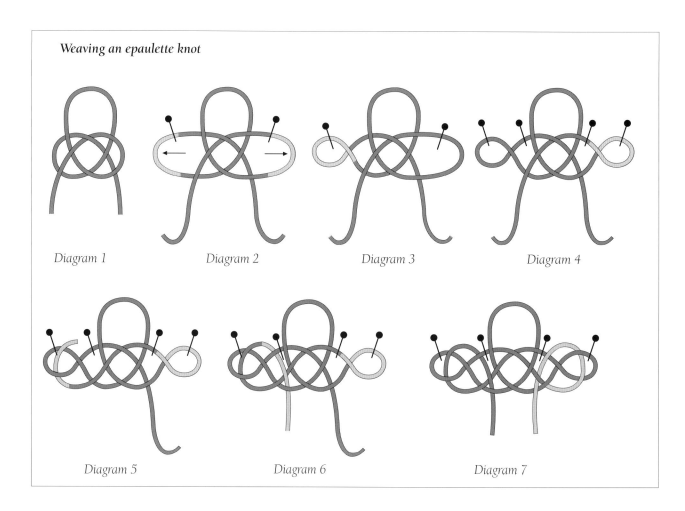

| Diagram 1 | Diagram 2 | Diagram 3 | Diagram 4 |

| Diagram 5 | Diagram 6 | Diagram 7 |

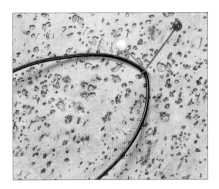

1. Find the centre of the first piece of leather cord and place it on the cork mat. Hold it in place with two pins crossed as shown so that the pins can not damage the leather.

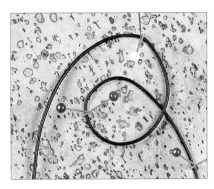

2. Make a loop with the right-hand end of the cord with the free end going underneath and pin it as before.

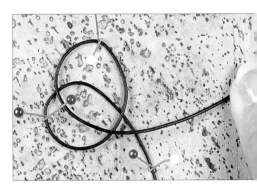

3. Take the left-hand end of the cord over the loop.

Note

It is extremely important that the lace goes over and under the correct parts of the cord when the knot is woven. Make frequent references to the diagrams to make sure that each stage is correct.

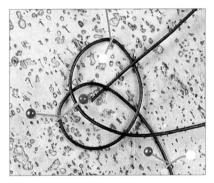

4. Take the left-hand end (which is now on the right-hand side) up to the right then down and weave it over and under the cord as shown.

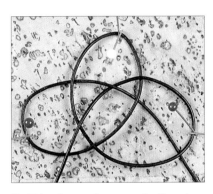

5. Take the cord over and off to the left to make the shape shown. See diagram 1. Note that the unders and overs vary from the basic Josephine knot (see page 15).

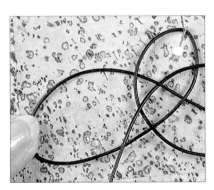

6. Remove the pins on the left and ease the loop out. See diagram 2.

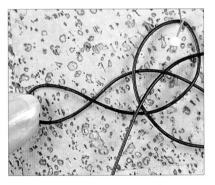

7. Twist the left loop up and over itself. See diagram 3.

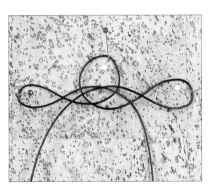

8. Pin the loop in place and then twist the loop on the right-hand side down and over itself. See diagram 4.

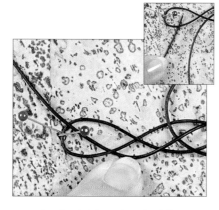

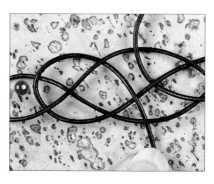

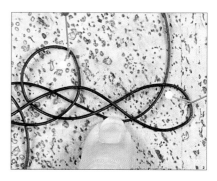

9. Take the left-hand end of the cord under the left-hand twisted loop (see inset). Pull the end through to the top left while holding the cord in place as shown in the main photograph. See diagram 5.

10. Take the end under, over and under the cord as shown to lock the leather in position on the left. See diagram 6.

11. Take the right-hand end over and through the rightmost loop, as shown; working the opposite overs and unders to the side you have completed. Remember to hold the cord in place.

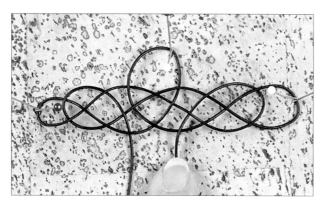

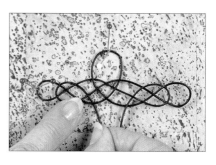

12. Take the end over, under and over the cord as shown to lock the leather. See diagram 7. This completes an epaulette knot.

13. Starting from the middle of the knot, gradually work around the cord, tightening it.

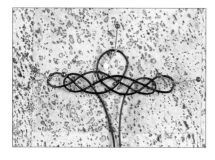

Note

When tightening, remember to work in short stages, gradually making the knot as a whole smaller and tighter.

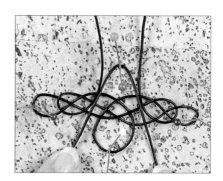

14. Continue tightening the knot until it measures roughly 5cm (2in).

15. Turn your cork mat around and pin the second length of leather on the mat as shown. Starting at what is now the top of the knot will ensure that the second cord will start and end in the opposite direction to the first one.

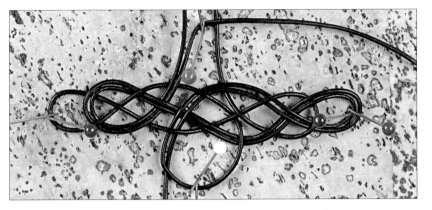

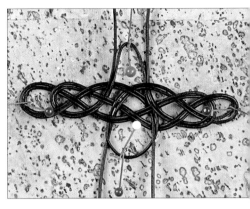

16. Following the path of the first length of cord, weave the left-hand end of the new cord around the knot.

17. Weave the right-hand end of the new length around the knot, following the path of the first knot.

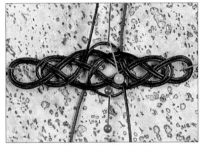

18. Gradually tighten the knot. Because there are two cords going in opposite directions, tighten each cord simultaneously at each point by pulling one cord in one direction and the other in the opposite direction. This is painstaking but worth the effort.

19. Continue tightening until the work is roughly half its original size. Remove the pins as necessary while you are tightening the knot. This completes a double epaulette knot.

20. Thread one of the beads on to the leather cords below the knot.

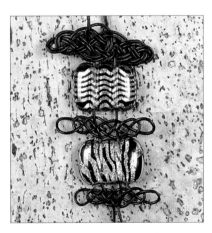

21. Carefully anchor the double knot and bead with a pin or two, then make a single epaulette knot below the bead.

22. Tighten the knot, then slip a second bead on to the ends of the cord.

23. Make a third epaulette knot and tighten it a little more than the previous knot to ensure it is smaller.

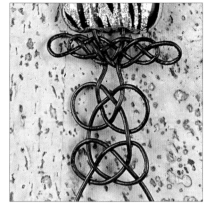

24. Pin the right-hand end of the cord out of the way. Make a loop with the left-hand end of the cord (with the free end going over the other cord) and pin it in place.

25. Unpin the right-hand end and then take it under the top of the loop, then weave it alternately over and under, bringing it up, over and down to the right to make a Josephine knot as shown.

26. Tighten the Josephine knot, then make a second Josephine knot as a mirror of the first (i.e. the unders and overs are the opposite to the first knot. Start with the right-hand end). This will ensure that the bracelet lies flat and does not twist around on itself.

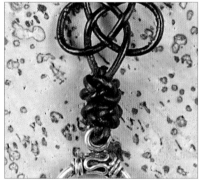

28. Adjust the button knots so that they are adjacent, then trim the excess cord. Secure the knots with a touch of superglue gel if necessary.

27. Take the two ends through the loop of the clasp and make two sliding button knots to secure the loop in place.

29. Repeat from step 20 on the other end of the bracelet, substituting the toggle for the loop to finish the bracelet.

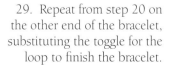

Opposite:

A double epaulette knot surrounded by amber beads was used for the topmost necklace, while wooden beads and a central polymer clay bead with a picture of a Japanese lady was used for the second variation at the bottom of the picture. This bead was made by Eileen Loring of Colorado in the United States.

The black and silver dichroic beads used in the project bracelet were made by glass artist Janet Wollery.

44

FIRECRACKER KNOT EARRINGS

Firecrackers in China are believed to frighten away evil spirits. I first saw these knots in many different colours in an elaborate Chinese decorative hanging, combined with a fearsome lion dog's head and several different Chinese knots.

This hanging is illustrated in my Chinese knot book and so many people asked me how to make the firecracker knot that I decided to include it here. When the ends are left free they make a lovely tassel, known as the Tassel of Good Fortune, and make elegant earrings.

The firecracker knot is also known as a crown knot, and one single knot (as in diagram 4, below) is known as a Japanese bend.

You will need

Ten 60cm (24in) lengths of gold 1mm satin cord

Two feature beads

A pair of earring hooks

Weaving a firecracker knot

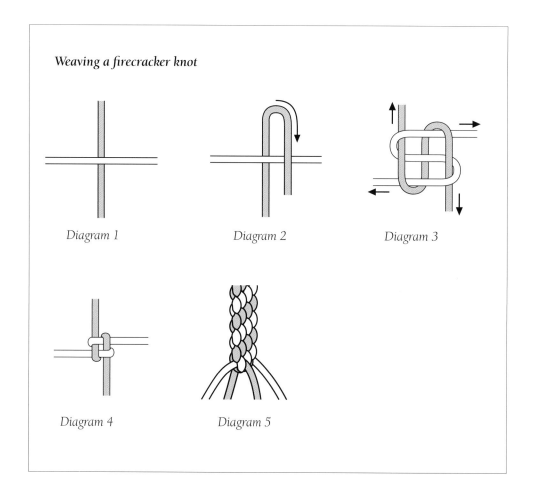

Diagram 1

Diagram 2

Diagram 3

Diagram 4

Diagram 5

46

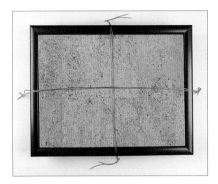

1. Take two lengths of gold cord and lay them vertically across your cork mat. Lay another pair of gold cords horizontally to make a cross. See diagram 1.

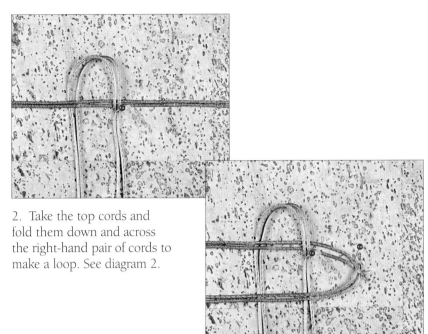

2. Take the top cords and fold them down and across the right-hand pair of cords to make a loop. See diagram 2.

3. Take the right-hand cords and fold them across the cords at the bottom, making a loop on the right side.

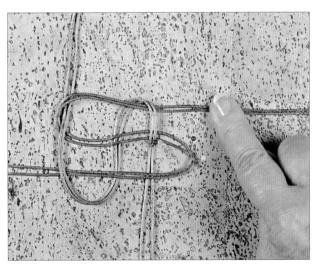

4. Take the left-hand pair of cords at the bottom, and fold them across the cords at the left.

5. Take the upper pair of cords on the left and fold them across the pair currently pointing upwards, then take them over and through the loop as shown. See diagram 3.

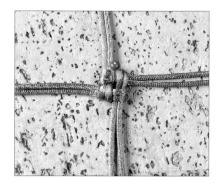

6. Gradually tighten the knot. You will find pinning the centre makes this easier. See diagram 4.

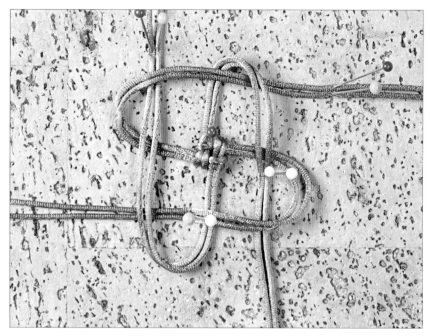

7. Repeat steps 2–5 to make the shape shown.

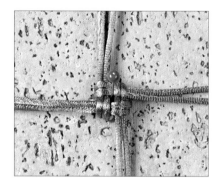

8. Tighten the cords so that they lie on top of the previous knot.

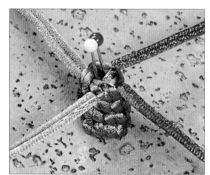

9. Repeat the process four more times so that you have a stack of six knots on top of one another.

10. Remove the knot from the corkboard and apply a dab of instant glue gel to the centre of the knot at the top.

11. Thread a needlepoint needle with a length of gold cord and take it through the two loops at the bottom of the knot (note that this will later become the top of the knot). Remove the needle from the cord.

12. Hold both ends of the new cord together and thread a bead down them to the knot.

13. Thread the earring hook on to the cord.

14. Use one of the cords round the other three cords to tie a button knot under the earring hook, following the instructions on pages 19–20. Move the button knot up next to the earring hook.

15. Trim and seal the loose ends of the cord coming from the button knot.

16. Make a tube by rolling up a 3.5 x 6cm (1½ x 2½in) piece of plastic acetate. Secure it with a small piece of sticky tape.

17. Dampen the tassel, slip it inside the tube and allow to dry.

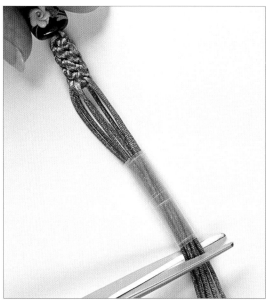

18. Run the tube down the tassel to the length desired, then use it as a guide to cut the tassel to length.

19. Make a second earring in the same way.

Pink and white 'Kimono' glass beads made by Rachelle Goldreich were used in both the necklace and the pink earrings, while I used blue-white and gold lampwork beads for the project. These were also made by Rachelle.

PIPA KNOT EARRINGS

A pipa is a Chinese string instrument rather like a lute. This knot is named after the pipa as it has the same shape. The shape also gives it the alternative name 'teardrop knot'.

Take your pick of which name you like better! Whatever you call it, this knot has a lovely graceful shape and is particularly good for earrings.

You will need

Two 60cm (24in) lengths of turquoise 1mm leather cord

Two 50cm (18in) lengths of turquoise 1mm satin cord

A pair of earring hooks

Two large and four small beads

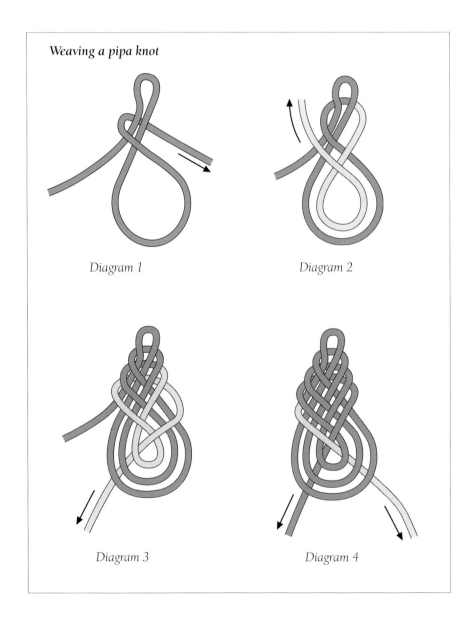

Weaving a pipa knot

Diagram 1

Diagram 2

Diagram 3

Diagram 4

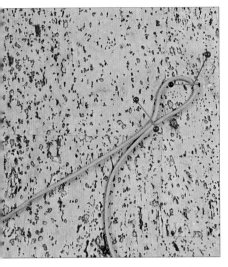

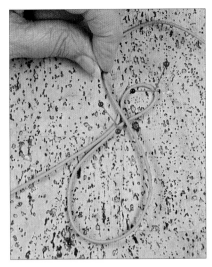

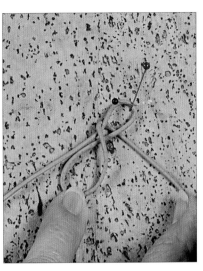

1. Secure the 60cm (24in) leather cord to the cork mat. Pin either side of the leather as shown to avoid spoiling it. Curl the leather round into an uncrossed loop, leaving a 10cm (4in) tail on the left-hand end.

2. Bring the right-hand end of the cord around and up to make a large lower loop. Lay it across the intersection of the two loops as shown.

3. Wrap the cord behind the top loop to make a flat coil around the intersection of the two loops. See diagram 1.

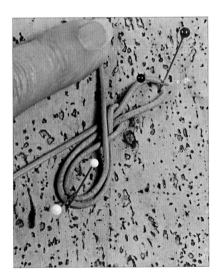

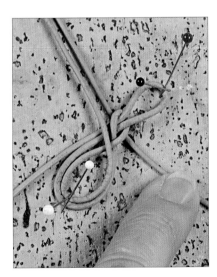

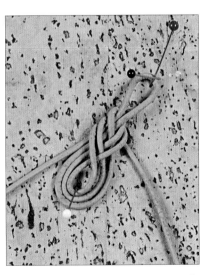

4. Bring the cord down, around and up again to make a smaller loop within the lower loop. See diagram 2.

5. Wrap it around and behind the intersection again, taking care that it curls inside and below the first coil.

6. Bring the cord down and around again to make a third loop inside the first two, then up again, around and behind to curl inside and below the previous coil.

53

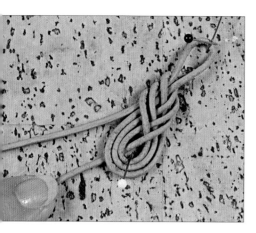  

7. Take the right-hand end and thread it through the centre of the lower loops. See diagram 3.

8. Take the left-hand end across the left side of the loops, over the newly threaded cord, then down through the hole in the centre and under the right side. See diagram 4.

9. Remove the knot from the cork mat, turn it over and secure the loose ends on the back with a dab of instant glue gel. Cut the excess cord off.

12. Make a second earring in the same way to complete the pair.

10. Thread the 50cm (18in) cord through the loop at the top, then thread a large bead sandwiched between two small beads on to the new cord.

11. Slide one of the earring hooks on to the new cord (see inset), then tie a button knot with one end of the new cord around the other. Move the hook and knot into place, then trim the excess cord.

Opposite:

The necklace uses a single pipa knot as a decorative pendant, while the cord is made up of button knots in 1mm purple satin cord, interspersed with a mix of ceramic, glass and silver beads.

Both sets of earrings use ceramic and mixed glass beads to complement pipa knots made from leather cord.

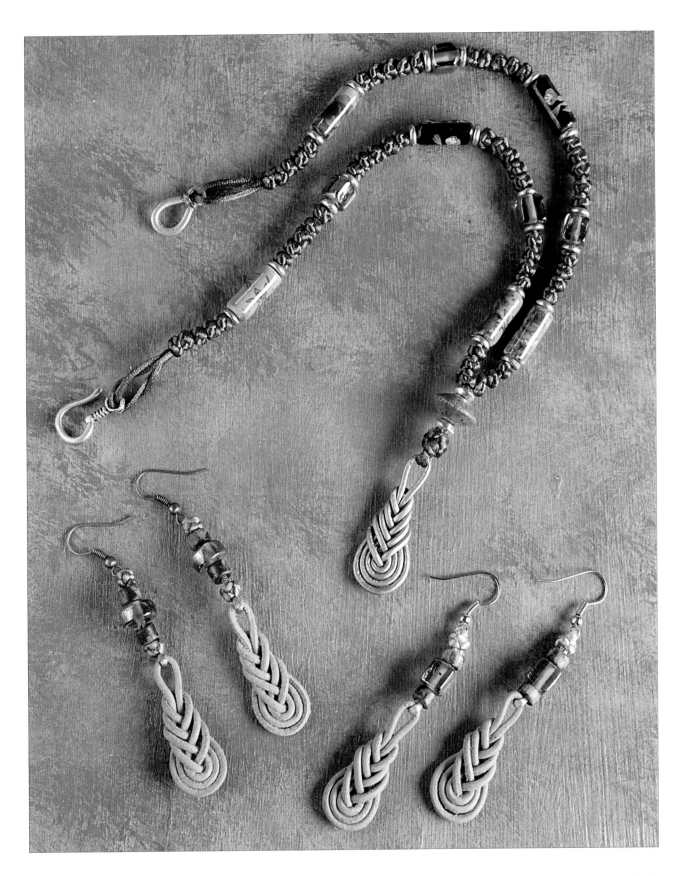

MACRAMÉ NECKLACE

This knot is known as a square knot in macramé, and the Chinese call it a flat knot. The ancient Egyptians and Greeks called it a Hercules knot, so it has a long and varied history.

In the 1970s macramé was very popular and mostly made with string and hemp. These days macramé is enjoying a revival, but since it is now generally made with much finer cords in vibrant colours, the finished pieces look much more sophisticated.

In parts of this necklace, only the first half of the square knot is tied repeatedly, and this causes the cords to twist, making a spiral knot. This knot is also very attractive, especially if the cord is shiny.

You will need

4.5m (177in) purple 1mm satin cord
1m (36in) purple 1mm satin cord
30cm (12in) purple 1mm satin cord
Silver-coloured toggle closure
Large flower bead (or similar large decorative bead)
Five small white beads
One pearl bead

Weaving a square knot

Diagram 1

Diagram 2

Diagram 3

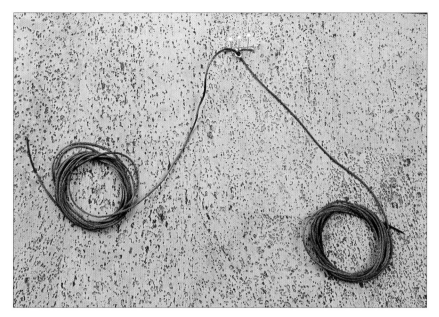

1. Slide the toggle closure up to the centre of the 4.5m (177in) purple cord and pin it to the board. These will be the knotting cords.

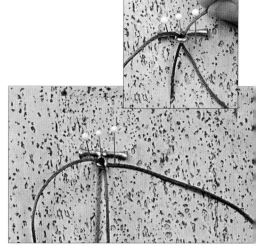

2. Slide the 1m (36in) purple cord through the toggle (see inset), then pull it through to the centre and run both ends down the board as shown. These are the 'lazy cords' (also known as 'core').

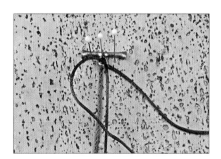

3. Take the left-hand knotting cord over the lazy cords, making a loop on the left.

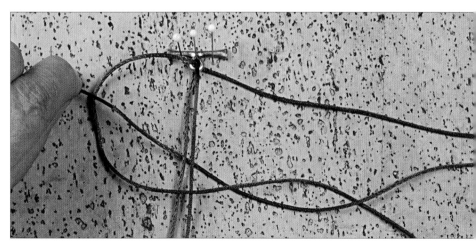

4. Take the right-hand knotting cord over the left-hand knotting cord, under the lazy cords and up through the loop on the left.

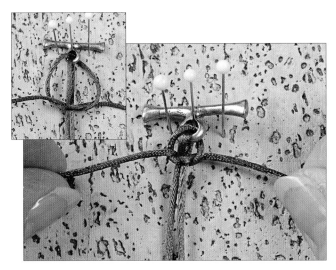

5. Pull the right-hand cord through (see inset), and tighten the knot. See diagram 1.

Note

This is the first half of the knot. If it is repeatedly tied, a spiral knot is made.

6. Take the cord on the right over the lazy cords, making a loop on the right.

Tip

When making the square knot remember that the second cord goes 'over, under and up'. This will help you build up a natural rhythm.

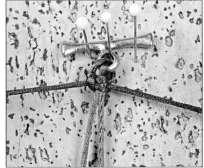

7. Take the knotting cord on the left over the other knotting cord, under the lazy cords and up through the loop as shown.

8. Pull the cord through the loop and tighten. See diagram 2. You have now completed one square knot.

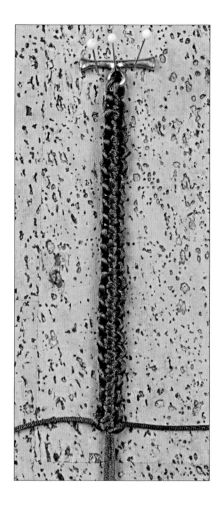

9. Repeat the process from step 3 until the knots form a 12cm (4¾in) length.

10. Thread a white bead on to both lazy cords and run it up to the last square knot as shown.

11. This next section is made up of spiral knots, made in the following way: take the left-hand knotting cord over the lazy cords, making a loop.

12. Take the right-hand knotting cord over the knotting cord, under the lazy cords and up through the loop on the left.

13. Tighten the knot (see inset), then repeat from step 11 until the knots form a 7.5cm (3in) length. Note that if only the first half of the square knot (left over right) is repeated (rather than alternating left over right with right over left, as in the square knot), the knots will twist into a spiral. These are called spiral knots.

Tip

The tendency of spiral knots to twist is so strong that the work will spiral. Once you find the twist makes working difficult, simply turn the work over in the direction of the twist, pull the knotting cords round and continue.

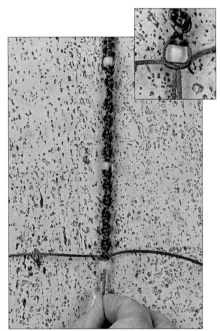

14. Secure a bead at the bottom of the spiral knots as before (see inset), then work another 7.5cm (3in) of spiral knots and thread on a third bead.

15. Secure the bead as before and work 12cm (4¾in) of square knots.

16. Unpin the work and place it on scrap paper with the working end at the top as shown. Thread the loop closure on to the lazy cords 1cm (½in) from the square knots.

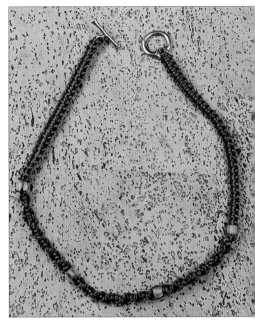

17. Fold the lazy cords over and cut them so that the ends reach the square knots (see inset), then glue the lazy cords down on themselves using instant glue gel.

18. When the glued cords are secure, pin the piece back on the cork board then work square knots over the glued piece as shown.

19. Trim and seal the ends to complete the basic necklace.

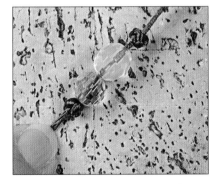

20. To make the pendant, set the necklace to one side, then make a button knot at one end of the 30cm (12in) cord. Thread on the two crystal beads and secure them in place with a second button knot.

21. Make a small overhand knot by taking the cord over itself 1cm (½in) above the button knot to hold the flower bead in place, then thread on the large flower bead.

22. Thread on the pearl bead, then take the end of the cord through the top of the flower bead so the bead sits in the centre of the flower. Pull the cord through and thread on the last small white bead.

Note

If it is not possible to find an identical large flower bead, substitute your own pendant for a different tassel. Do not worry: enjoy the creativity of making your own design!

61

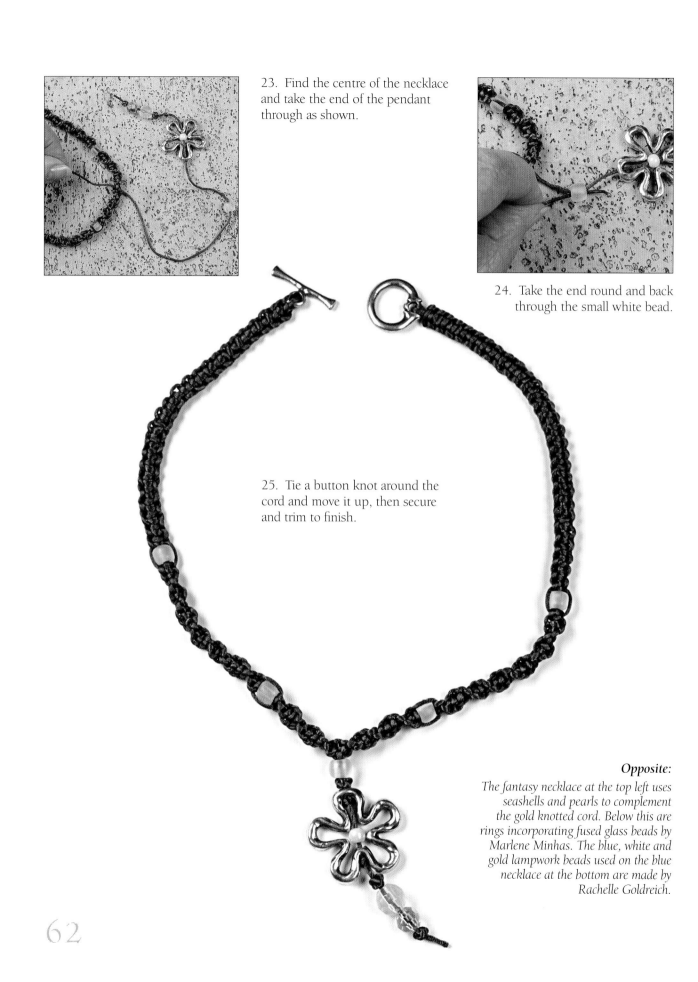

23. Find the centre of the necklace and take the end of the pendant through as shown.

24. Take the end round and back through the small white bead.

25. Tie a button knot around the cord and move it up, then secure and trim to finish.

Opposite:

The fantasy necklace at the top left uses seashells and pearls to complement the gold knotted cord. Below this are rings incorporating fused glass beads by Marlene Minhas. The blue, white and gold lampwork beads used on the blue necklace at the bottom are made by Rachelle Goldreich.

FOUR-LEAVED CLOVER NECKLACE

Finding a four-leaved clover is considered to be very lucky both in China and the West. However if you can not find one, here is how to make one of your own! This knot is tied in a similar way to a cloverleaf knot but with an extra leaf.

    When it is finished it will need a couple of tiny drops of instant glue gel in the centre to hold it firmly, especially if it is made with satin cord.

You will need

One glass pendant

Two black beads and three decorative glass beads

60cm (24in) black 2mm satin cord

270cm (106in) black 2mm satin cord

270cm (106in) gold 2mm satin cord

A number of 30cm (12in) lengths of black 2mm satin cord

A number of 30cm (12in) lengths of gold 2mm satin cord

Fish and toggle closure

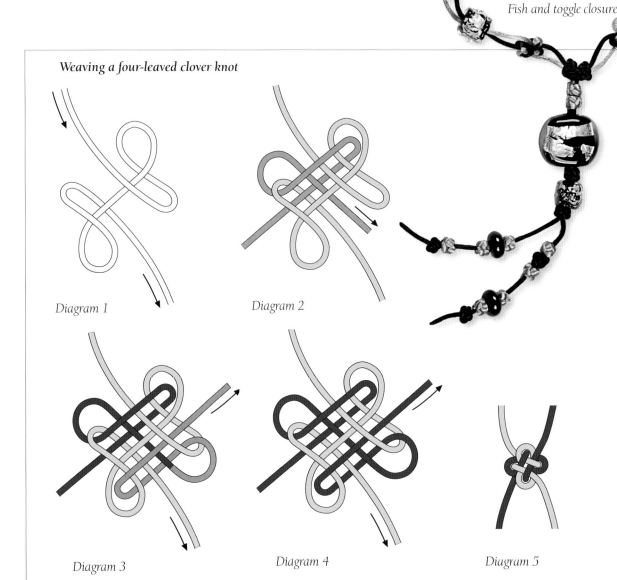

Weaving a four-leaved clover knot

Diagram 1

Diagram 2

Diagram 3

Diagram 4

Diagram 5

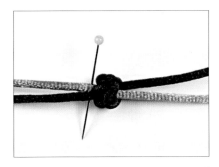

2. Remove the anchor pin and tie a second button knot with the other end of the black cord around the gold cord. Move it up next to the other knot.

1. Lay the 270cm (106in) black and gold cords next to each other and place a pin through the centre of both cords to act as an anchor. Tie a button knot with the black cord around the gold cord and move it up to the pin (see page 16).

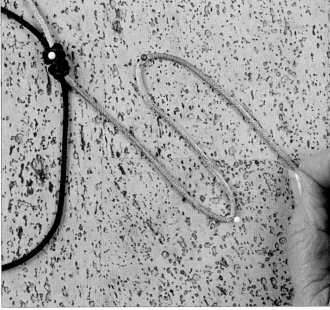

3. Pin the piece to the corkboard, then pin the gold cord into a wide 'S' shape as shown.

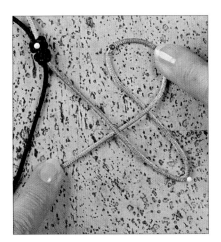

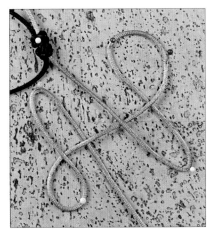

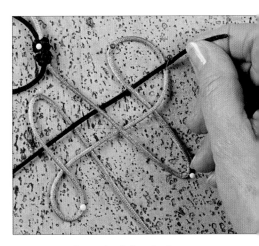

4. Take the end over then under the cord and draw through to make a loop at the top.

5. Pin the top loop, then make a second loop at the bottom. Pin and then make a doubled-back loop taking the end first over then under the cord as shown. See diagram 1.

6. Starting from the left side (as shown in diagram 2), take the black cord under the gold cord, over it, and then under twice and up through the loop at the top.

65

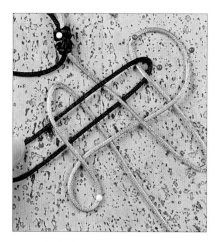

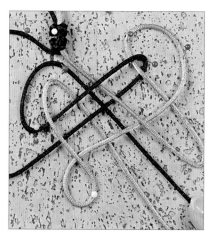

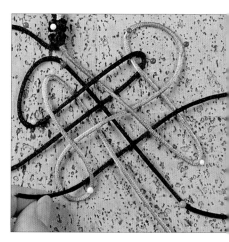

7. Pull the black cord up through the loop, then pin and weave it down over the first three cords and under the fourth.

8. Take it up and around to the right, then bring it down between the gold cords: under the first, over the second and under the third.

9. Take the black cord up to the right, then around to the left and down. Weave it over the first cord, under the next four and up through the gold loop.

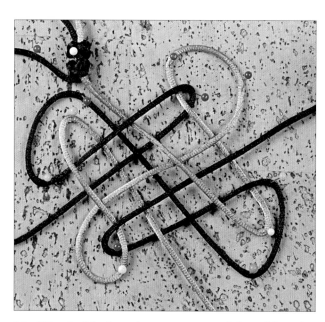

10. Take the black cord over two parts of the gold cord (see picture), over the black cord, under the gold cord and then over the last gold cord. Pull through to finish the weaving of the knot. (see diagram 3).

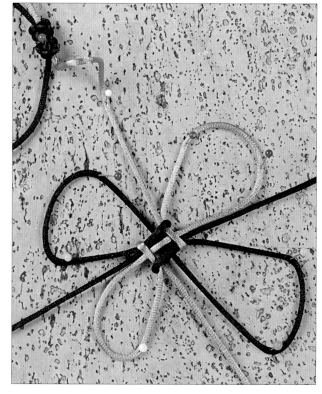

11. Begin to tighten the knot by removing pins and pulling the loose ends (as shown in diagram 4) until the centre of the knot is formed as shown.

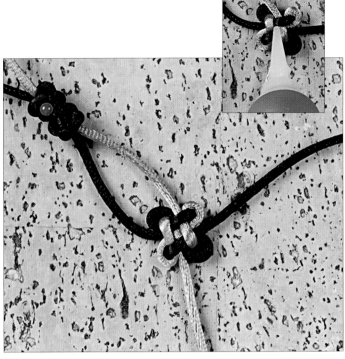

12. Continue to tighten the knot, being careful to ensure that the loops do not flip over out of place, as this will ruin the knot. They will flip over if not held down. See diagram 5.

13. Very carefully and gradually, move the knot up the gold cord towards the button knots and re-tighten 2cm (¾in) from the button knots. Add a dab of instant glue gel to secure the centre of the knot (see inset).

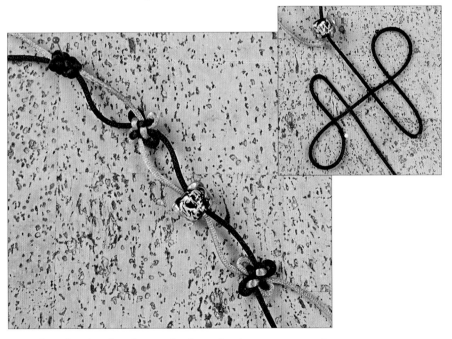

14. Thread a glass bead on to both cords, then tie a second four-leaved clover knot. Start with the black cord rather than the gold (see inset), and move it up to the bead, tightening it 2cm (1in) below it.

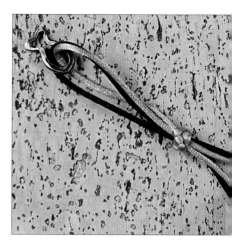

15. Leave a gap of 2cm (1in), then tie three button knots around the black cord using the gold cord.

16. Tie three button knots around the gold cord using the black cord.

17. Slide the fish loop on to the cords and double the cords over. Tie a button knot with the gold cord around the three other cords to secure it in place.

18. Tie a black knot around the three other cords. Cut and seal the loose ends to complete the first half of the necklace. You have two sliding knots next to each other, making the finish less bulky than a double button knot using both cords.

19. Work the second half in the same way as the first, following steps 37, replacing the fish loop with a toggle.

20. To make the pendant, take the 60cm (24in) black cord. Fold the cord slightly off-centre so that one end is approximately 5cm (2in) shorter than the other, and make a loop large enough to slip over the beads on the necklace and tie a button knot using one end of the cord around the other.

21. Slide the glass pendant over the loop down to the button knot, then use a pin to anchor it.

22. Slide a glass bead on to both free ends and slide it up to the button knots. Secure it in place with a second button knot.

23. On the longer end of the cord, make a button knot 5cm (2in) down from the previous knot. Thread on a black bead, then tie another button knot near the end of the cord.

24. Thread a black bead on to the shorter end of the cord, then tie a button knot near the end of the cord.

Tip
These knots are tied on to the black cords in the same way as any other button knots, except that each has two loose ends to trim to make the knot.

25. Thread the pendant's loop on to the necklace so that it sits in the centre between the original black button knots (see step 2).

26. Use the short lengths of gold cord to tie as many button knots as necessary in the space between the button knots on the necklace and the large black and gold pendant bead.

The finished necklace.

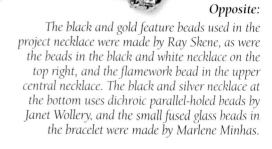

Opposite:
The black and gold feature beads used in the project necklace were made by Ray Skene, as were the beads in the black and white necklace on the top right, and the flamework bead in the upper central necklace. The black and silver necklace at the bottom uses dichroic parallel-holed beads by Janet Wollery, and the small fused glass beads in the bracelet were made by Marlene Minhas.

DRAGONFLY BROOCH

Dragonflies have long been admired for their delicate lacy wings, iridescent colour and fanciful, unpredictable flight. One legend has it that dragonflies are 'dragons' grandchildren' as they are believed to emerge from the cast-off skin of dragons. Chinese people believe that harming or trapping a dragonfly causes illness.

The knot is made from two cords tied as one to make a large button knot head, and a virtue knot to make the wings, then using the four cords a series of flat knots make the body. I like to leave a trailing tail but you can trim the cord at the end of the body if you prefer.

You will need

175cm (69in) royal blue 1mm braided cord

175cm (69in) turquoise 1mm braided cord

Brooch pin

Black leather

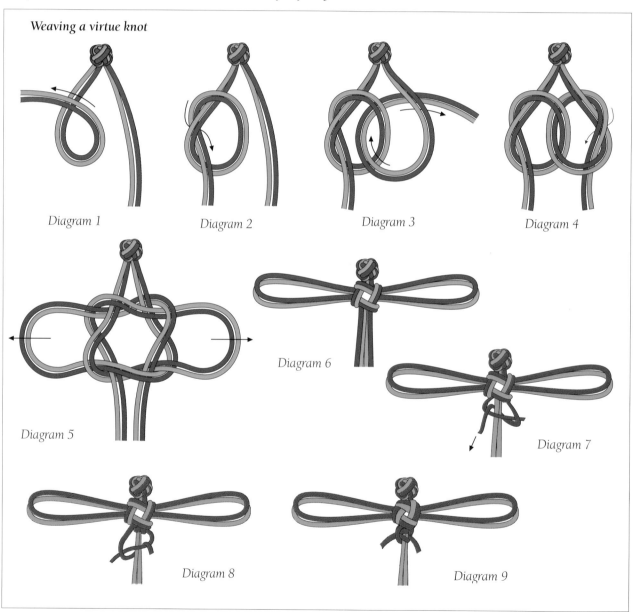

Weaving a virtue knot

Diagram 1

Diagram 2

Diagram 3

Diagram 4

Diagram 5

Diagram 6

Diagram 7

Diagram 8

Diagram 9

72

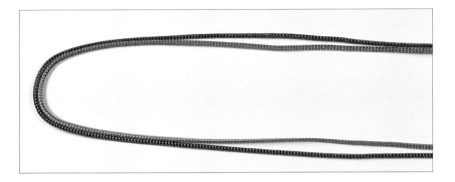

1. Lie both cords down alongside each other and find the centre.

2. Using the paired cords as one cord, tie a button knot by tying one pair of cords around the other pair and moving the knot to the centre.

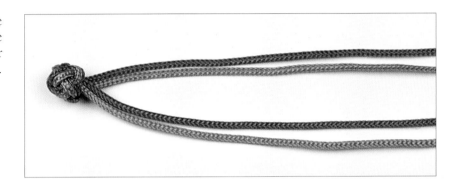

3. Place the piece on your corkboard and place a pin through the button knot. Take one cord of each colour to either side.

4. Using the cords on the left, make a loop as shown. Keep the cords parallel and do not let them cross over each other (see diagram 1).

5. Take the ends underneath and through the loop to make an overhand knot (see diagram 2).

6. Take the paired ends on the right through the loop of the overhand knot, and then under itself to make a loop on the right (see diagram 3).

7. Take the ends underneath and through the loop to make a second overhand knot on the right.

8. The twists on the outsides of the loops make figures of eight (see diagram 4). Use a pair of tweezers to reach in through the top of the figure of eight on the left-hand side and grip the inside of the right-hand overhand knot as shown.

9. Carefully pull the gripped piece through the top of the figure of eight.

10. Repeat on the other side. Make sure that none of the cords have crossed over each other (see diagram 5).

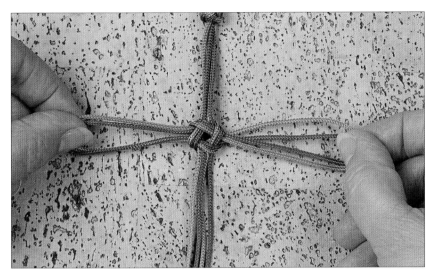

11. Carefully pull the loops out to form the virtue knot, but do not tighten it completely.

12. Ease the virtue knot up into position beneath the button knot to form the head and abdomen of the dragonfly.

13. Ease the cords through until the wingspan is roughly 8cm (3¼in). Tighten the knot to complete the virtue knot.

14. With the virtue knot in place, we will now make the square knot tail. Arrange the cords at the bottom as shown, with the turquoise as the knotting cords and the royal blue cords as the lazy cords.

15. Take the left-hand knotting cord over the lazy cords to make a loop.

Tip
See page 56 for the square knot diagrams.

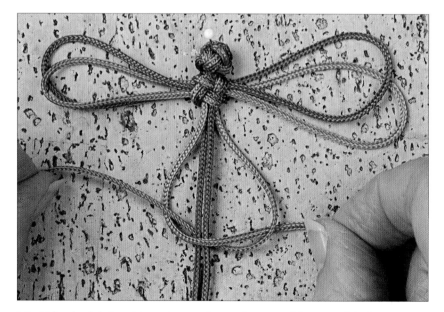

16. Take the left-hand knotting cord over the central 'lazy cords', then take the right-hand cord over the left-hand cord, under the lazy cords and up through the loop as shown.

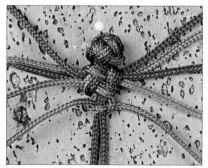

17. Gently tighten the knot so it sits underneath the abdomen.

Tip

Remember that for square knots, the second cord goes 'over, under and up'; and that the same knotting cord should always remain on top.

18. Take the right-hand knotting cord over the lazy cords, then take the left-hand knotting cord over the right-hand knotting cord, under the lazy cords and up through the loop.

19. Tighten the knot to complete one square knot.

20. Gradually making the knots tighter (and hence smaller) as you continue, work square knots until the thorax is 7cm (3in) long.

21. Remove the anchor pin and trim and seal the turquoise cords. Trim and seal the royal blue cords to approximately 5cm (2in) as shown.

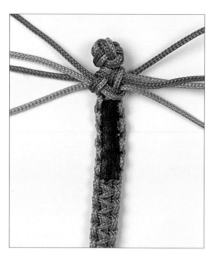

22. Secure a strip of leather to the back of the dragonfly with a little instant glue gel.

23. Once dry, glue the brooch pin back on to the leather.

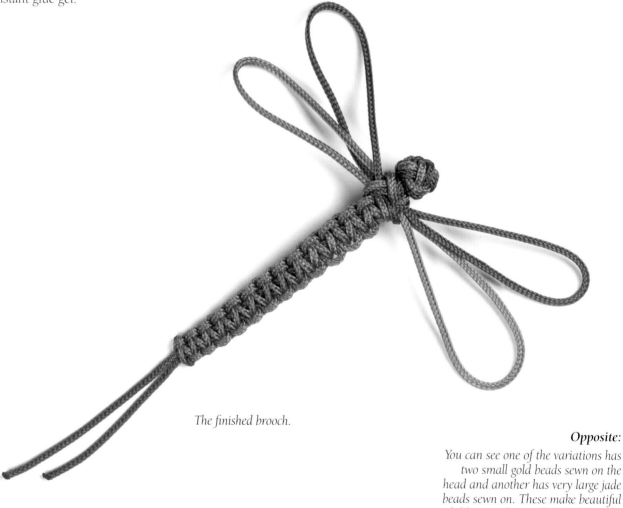

The finished brooch.

Opposite:
You can see one of the variations has two small gold beads sewn on the head and another has very large jade beads sewn on. These make beautiful orb-like eyes that really help bring the dragonfly to life.

INDEX

anchor pin 15, 64, 77

ball beads 22, 25
bar beads 34, 37
beads 9, 10, 11, 16, 17, 18, 19, 20, 22, 26, 32, 34, 43, 49, 52, 54, 56, 59, 60, 61, 62, 64, 69, 70, 78
bracelet 15, 20, 21, 22, 25, 26, 40, 44, 70
braided cord 8, 72
brooch 72, 78
button knots 12, 16, 18, 19, 22, 25, 29, 31, 37, 38, 44, 49, 50, 54, 61, 62, 67, 69, 70, 73, 75
    sliding button knots 12, 16, 20, 38, 44, 68

calculating lengths of cord 12
Celtic 8, 16, 22, 26, 34
ceramic beads 9, 21, 26, 54
chain knot 28, 30, 31
Chinese 8, 16, 46, 56, 72
clasp 9, 16, 19, 22, 28, 31, 38, 40
    hook and eye 28, 29, 31, 38, 54
    toggle and loop 9, 16, 20, 22, 23, 25, 26, 41, 44, 57, 60, 65, 68
cloisonné beads 21
cords 8, 9, 12, 14, 17, 23, 24, 25, 26, 29, 30, 31, 32, 35, 36, 42, 43, 44, 47, 48, 62, 66
    synthetic cords 8, 10, 14
crown knot 46
cylinder beads 21

dragonfly 72, 75, 78
dragon's eye beads 22, 25, 34, 37
dyeing cords 14

earrings 46, 49, 50, 51, 52, 54
Egyptian 56
epaulette knot 15, 40, 43, 44

fabric beads 9
feature beads 21, 46
felt beads 9
firecracker knot 46
flat knot 56, 72
four-leaved clover knot 64, 67

glass beads 9, 21, 51, 54, 62, 64, 67, 69
    dichroic fused glass 9, 21, 40, 44, 70
Greek 56
Guinevere knot 34
    pattern 34, 35, 36, 37

instant glue gel 10, 26, 32, 48, 54, 61, 64, 67, 78

jewellery findings 9
Japanese bend 46
Josephine knot 15, 40, 41, 44

knotting cords 57, 58, 59, 76, 77

lampwork beads 9, 21, 26, 38, 51, 62
lazy cords 57, 58, 59, 60, 61, 76, 77
leather cord 8, 15, 38, 40, 41, 52, 53, 54
lighter 10

macramé 56

nail polish 11, 13
Native Americans 28
necklace 16, 19, 20, 28, 32, 34, 54, 56, 61, 62, 64, 68, 69, 70

overhand knot 73, 74

paper beads 9
pendants 9, 28, 31, 32, 34, 35, 36, 54, 61, 62, 64, 69, 70

pewter beads 9
pineapple knot 22, 25, 26
pipa knot 52, 54
plastic beads 9
pliers 11
polymer clay beads 9, 44
preparing cord ends 13

renaissance knot see Guinevere knot

satin cord 8, 13, 16, 22, 28, 34, 46, 52, 56
semi-precious stone beads 9
silver beads 9
sliding knots see button knots
spiral knot 58, 59, 60
square beads 22, 25
square knot 56, 58, 59, 60, 61, 76, 77
star-shaped beads 22, 25

teardrop knot 52
tension 25
thread zapper 10, 13
tightening 15, 16, 22, 36, 37, 42, 43, 60, 67, 75, 76
tubular beads 28, 29, 31
tweezers 10, 74

virtue knot 72, 75, 76

weaving 15, 16, 22, 28, 40, 46, 52, 56, 64, 66, 72
wire cutters 11
wooden beads 9, t 44